This

Nature Storybook

belongs to:

CW01582708

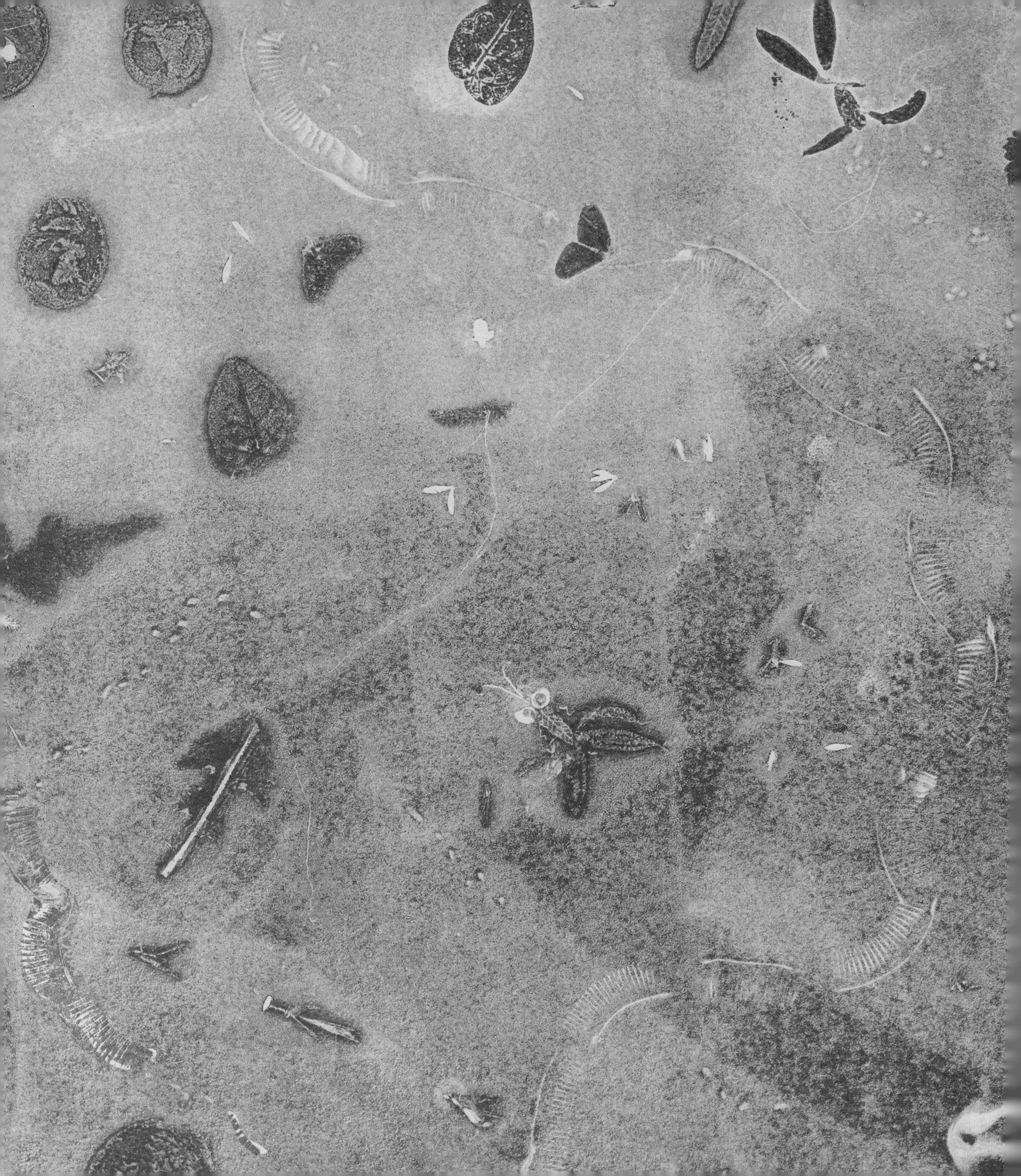

To Chloe, Aengus and Sarah, to remind you of Australia PF
Thank you to Mario for letting me explore LA

First published in 2016
by Walker Books Australia Pty Ltd
Locked Bag 22, Newtown
NSW 2042 Australia
www.walkerbooks.com.au

This edition published in 2018.

The moral rights of the author and illustrator have been asserted.

Text © 2016 Pamela Freeman
Illustrations © 2016 Liz Anelli

All rights reserved. No part of this publication may be reproduced, stored in a retrieval system, or transmitted in any form or by any means – electronic, mechanical, photocopying, recording or otherwise – without the prior written permission of the publisher.

National Library of Australia Cataloguing-in-Publication entry:
Freeman, Pamela, author.
Desert lake: The story of Kati Thanda–Lake Eyre / Pamela Freeman; illustrator: Liz Anelli.
ISBN: 978 1 760650 38 4 (paperback)
Series: Nature storybooks.
For children.
Subjects: Natural history – South Australia – Eyre, Lake, Region– Juvenile literature.
Botany – Australia, Central – Juvenile literature.
Zoology – Australia, Central – Juvenile literature.
Eyre, Lake (S.A.) – Juvenile literature.
Eyre, Lake, Region (S.A.) – Juvenile literature.
Australia, Central – Description and travel – Juvenile literature.
Other Authors/Contributors: Anelli, Liz, illustrator.

The illustrations for this book were created with mixed media

Typeset in Mrs Eaves, Mrs Ant and Gill Sans
Printed and bound in China

This project has been assisted by the Australia Council for the Arts Children's Picture Book Illustrators' Initiative, managed by the Australian Society of Authors.

Australian Government | Australia Council for the Arts | asa Australian Society of Authors

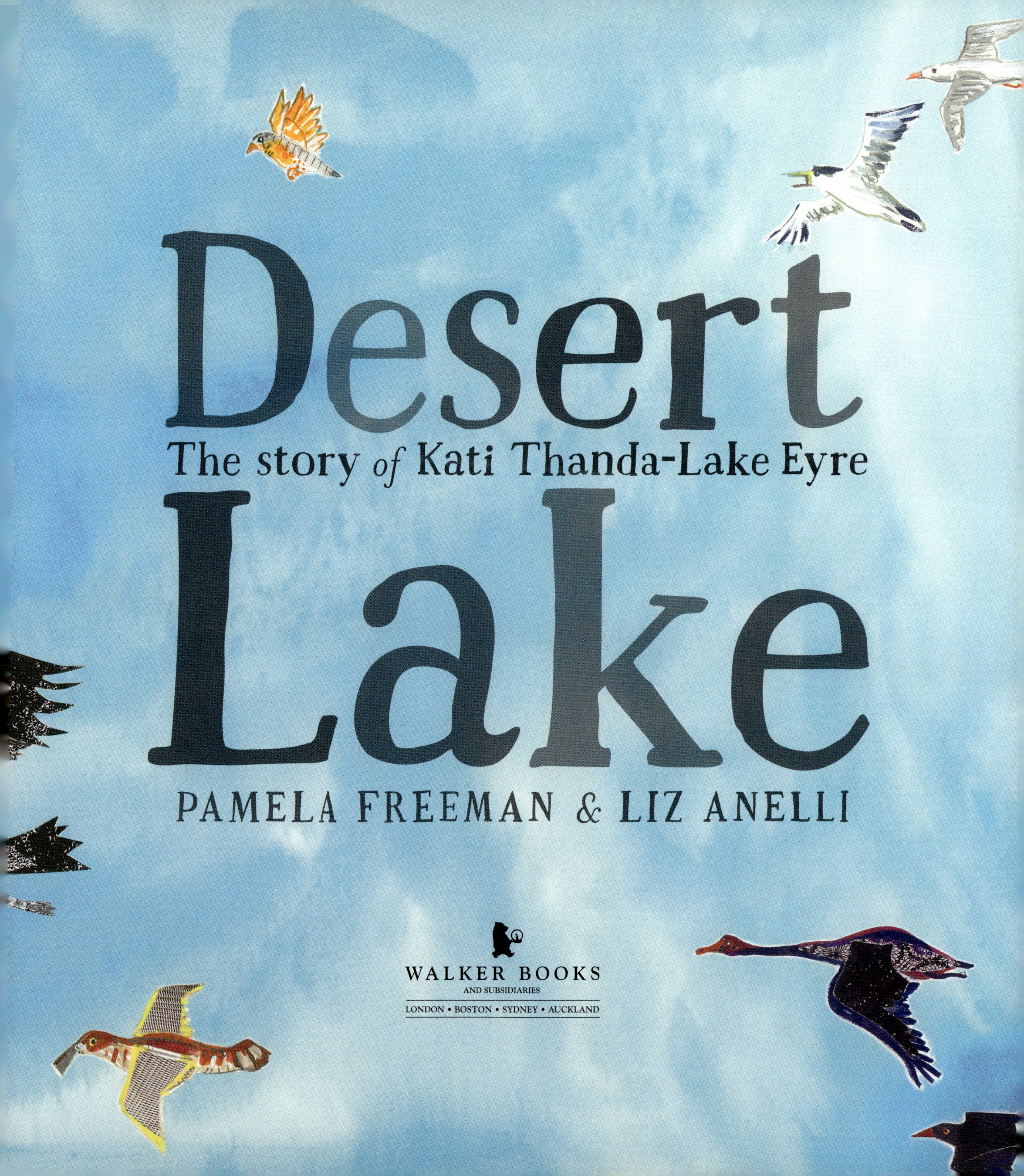

Desert Lake

The story *of* Kati Thanda-Lake Eyre

PAMELA FREEMAN & LIZ ANELLI

WALKER BOOKS
AND SUBSIDIARIES
LONDON • BOSTON • SYDNEY • AUCKLAND

Under the vast blue desert sky, the dry bed of Kati Thanda-Lake Eyre stretches to the horizon, blinding white with the salt of an ancient sea. The lake looks dead, but it's not.

Kati Thanda-Lake Eyre lies near the centre of Australia in a huge desert. The lake is usually dry but in some years the rains from the north flow to the lake area and create a mass of water.

Beneath the salt crust, frog and fish eggs are buried, waiting.
Frogs are safe in deep burrows, their heartbeats so slow
no one would know they are alive.

Below the lake bed, the frogs
can sleep for many years. They
live off fat and water stored
in their bodies.

But far up north, clouds are gathering: thunderheads and rain clouds.

Rain falls.

Rivers fill and break their banks.
And water **swirls** and **roars** down the
empty riverbeds towards the lake.

About every ten years the inland rivers flood into the lake. The water can flow at forty kilometres an hour – as fast as a galloping horse.

Basking in a billabong, a surprised fish is swept up in the flood and surges down the channel,

tumbling

and

leaping

as the wave carries it out onto the dry salt lake.

In some floods, the rivers have dumped eight *trillion* litres of fresh water into the lake. That is over three million Olympic swimming pools full of water. The fresh water mixes with the salt crust to form salty water, just like the ocean.

The water touches a buried frog. It wakes, blinking sleepy golden eyes at the newly wet world.

Nearby, the frogs' eggs, laid years ago for this very moment, float to the top of the new lake and hatch. Tadpoles wriggle away as fast as they can before the hungry gobies snap

them

up.

The frogs of Kati Thanda-Lake Eyre are special. Once they hatch, the tadpoles grow into frogs in just a few weeks.

Far, far away, pelicans **lift into the** sky – hundreds of them, heading for the lake to nest.

Their huge wings speed them across the great red desert to the one spot where their babies will be safe from dingoes and foxes – the new islands in the middle of the lake.

Pelicans fly as far as 1500 kilometres to come to the lake when it fills – some even fly across the Tasman Sea from New Zealand. No one understands how they know that the lake is full of water, but the pelicans don't come in years when the lake is dry.

The skies above the lake are alive with birds.

Shrieking gulls bring fish and insects to feed their babies, who are in woven grass nests **squawking** for food.

Two pink-eared ducks whistle to their ducklings to follow close, safe from the wedge-tailed eagle circling **high** above.

Pelicans and gulls both nest in colonies where hundreds of nests are clustered together on the ground. Smaller birds make nests in shrubs where they are safe from predators.

As the desert flames red and gold with sunset, tiny hopping mice **emerge from their burrows** on the lake shore while the dragon lizards **crawl wearily under their stones,** safe from the cold night air.

The mice and lizards live near
the lake all the time – and so do
humans! But many of the birds
come only when the lake is full.

Day after day, flocks of pelicans patrol the lake.

But the lake is shrinking.

Slowly, the harsh desert sun sucks the lake dry. The gusty winds steal tiny drops from the lake and carry them to become rain somewhere else. Each day the waters inch back a little further from the shore.

Once the initial flood is over, the rivers dry up. Then there is no more water feeding the lake. Water can stay in the lake for several years, growing gradually saltier and saltier as the surface water evaporates.

The frog that first woke, blinking, as the water touched her,
lays her eggs and then burrows into the cool deep earth,
closing her great golden eyes.

Plants also prepare for the dry period. Seaweed and algae release seeds and spores, and root-based plants die back. The seeds and roots, like the animals, can stay alive for years, waiting for the next flood.

The shield shrimps bury their tough eggs safely in the soft mud of the lake floor.

The pelican chicks are fully fledged, strong and eager to take to the uplands of the air, to ride the high winds to the great blue ocean. One day, they will come back to raise their own chicks here.

Below them, other birds leave too: avocets and gulls, ducks and swans.
The desert air is quiet, the lake that thrummed with life is still.
But some stay to keep watch over the lake.

The tiny zebra finches and the hunting birds – kites, wedge-tailed eagles and owls – love the desert in every season, and thrive in the dry air. They head out across the red plains to find other waterholes, springs and hidden billabongs.

Strong sun has baked the salt on the lake bed
into a crusty roof over the eggs and animals
hiding safe below ...
until the next time
the **rain**
falls.

About Kati Thanda-Lake Eyre

One hundred thousand years ago, the inland of Australia was a sea with many rivers feeding it. The climate became drier over time, and the sea became smaller and smaller, turning into a connected series of lakes, waterholes and rivers. Kati Thanda-Lake Eyre is the biggest of these. It is at the lowest point in Australia, and the rain from one-sixth of the continent drains into it. But since it now rains very rarely inland, the lake is usually dry.

Index

Look up the pages to find out all
about Kati Thanda-Lake Eyre things.
Don't forget to look at both kinds
of word – this kind and this kind.

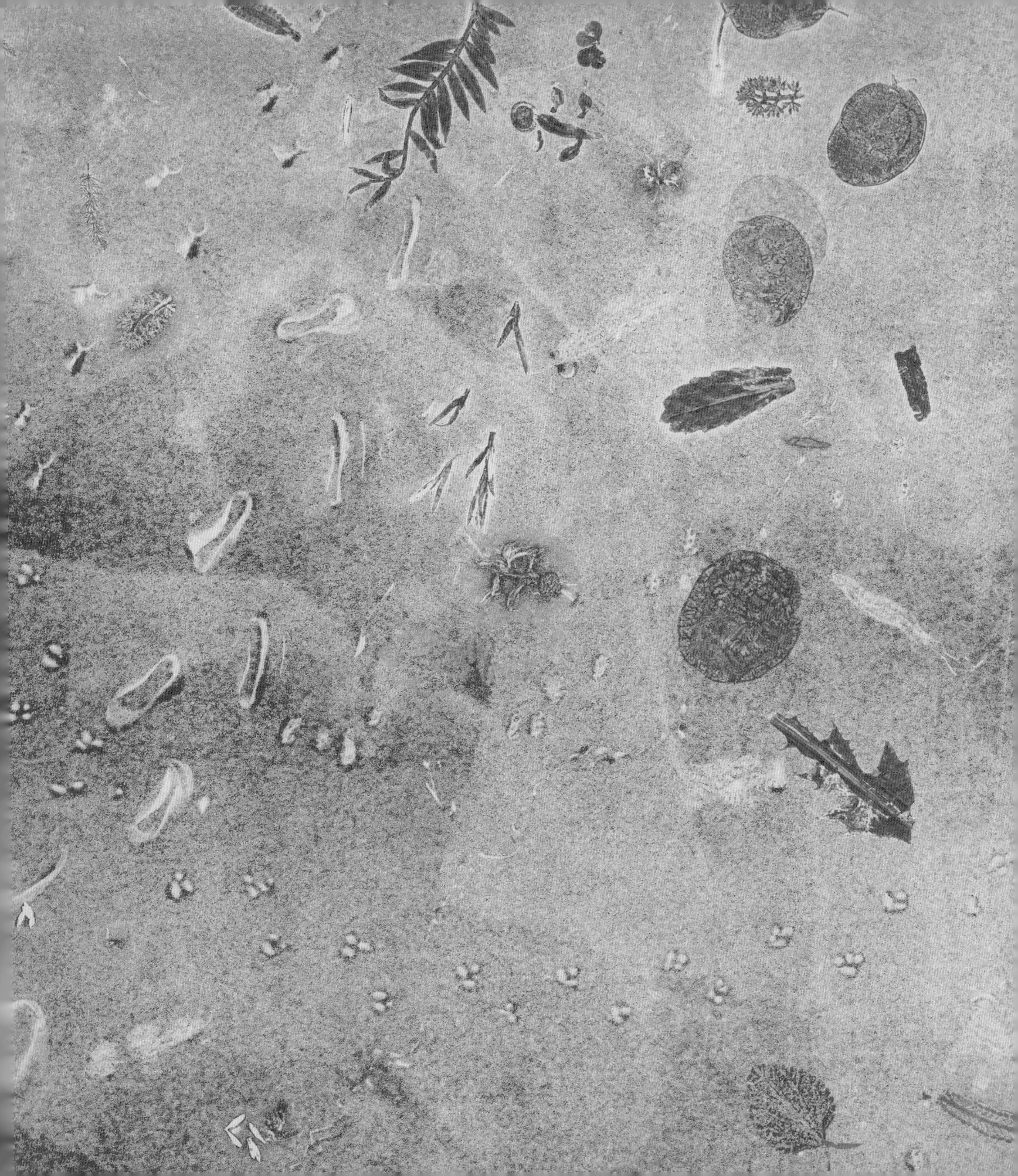

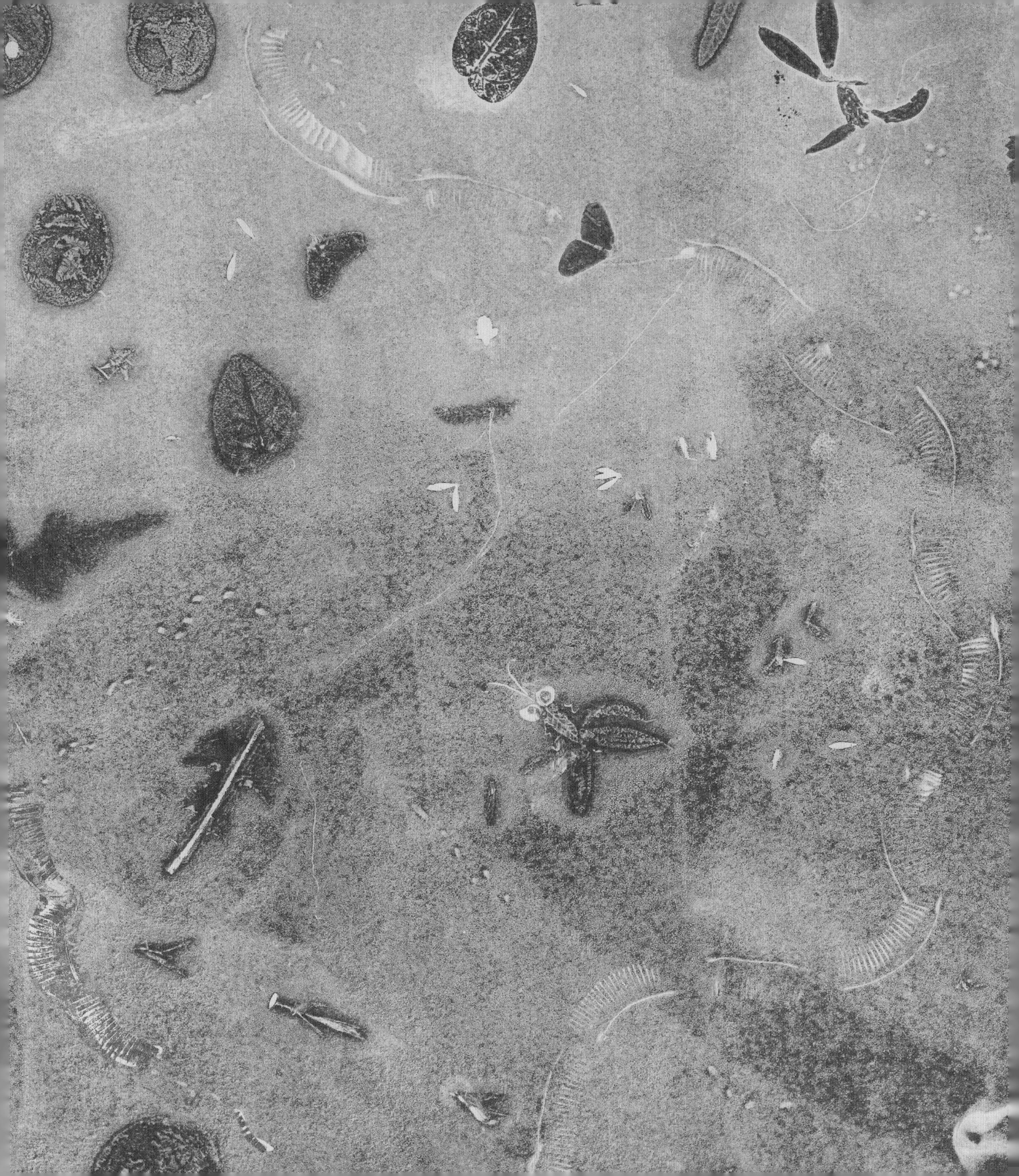

Nature Storybooks

BIG RED KANGAROO

by Claire Saxby
illustrated by Graham Byrne

WINNER, CRICHTON AWARD FOR NEW ILLUSTRATORS, CHILDREN'S BOOK COUNCIL OF AUSTRALIA BOOK OF THE YEAR AWARDS, 2014

"The combination of Claire Saxby's prose and debut illustrator Graham Byrne's pictures is an impressive marriage of extraordinary talent."
Magpies magazine

"An innovative addition to the children's nonfiction genre and a great way for children to learn about one of Australia's iconic animals."
Books+Publishing

Hardback 978-1-921720-42-0
Paperback 978-1-922244-39-0

PLATYPUS

by Sue Whiting
illustrated by Mark Jackson

NOTABLE BOOK, PICTURE BOOK CATEGORY, CHILDREN'S BOOK COUNCIL OF AUSTRALIA BOOK OF THE YEAR AWARDS, 2016

SHORTLISTED, NONFICTION CATEGORY, ENVIRONMENT AWARD FOR CHILDREN'S LITERATURE, 2016

NATIONAL SCIENCE TEACHERS ASSOCIATION OUTSTANDING TRADE SCIENCE BOOK, 2017 (US)

"Smoothly written and gently informative, this is a nice addition to the elementary-level nature shelf."
Kirkus Reviews

"The attractive picture book format encloses a readable, informative glimpse of one of the stranger creatures to be found on planet Earth."
School Library Journal

Paperback 978-1-925381-13-9

EMU

by Claire Saxby
illustrated by Graham Byrne

SHORT-LISTED, EVE POWNALL AWARD FOR INFORMATION BOOKS, CHILDREN'S BOOK COUNCIL OF AUSTRALIA BOOK OF THE YEAR AWARDS, 2015

WINNER, NONFICTION CATEGORY, ENVIRONMENT AWARD FOR CHILDREN'S LITERATURE, 2015

"Byrne's spiky digital illustrations perfectly display the emus' hairlike feathering and their awkward-looking flightless movement."
The Horn Book

Hardback 978-1-922179-70-8
Paperback 978-1-922077-15-8